SALA
& NEWTS

The color photograph on the cover was taken by Dr. P. Juster and is presented here through the courtesy of Ernst Leitz, manufacturers of the Leica camera. Photographs inside the book, unless specifically credited otherwise, are by the American Museum of Natural History or Laurence E. Perkins.

Mountain Salamander.

©Copyright 1977 by Dr. Herbert R. Axelrod

ISBN 0-87666-222-X

Distributed in the U.S.A. by T.F.H. Publications, Inc., 211 West Sylvania Avenue, P.O. Box 27, Neptune City, N.J. 07753; in England by T.F.H. (Gt. Britain) Ltd., 13 Nutley Lane, Reigate, Surrey; in Canada to the book store and library trade by Clarke, Irwin & Company, Clarwin House, 791 St. Clair Avenue West, Toronto 10, Ontario; in Canada to the pet trade by Rolf C. Hagen Ltd., 3225 Sartelon Street, Montreal 382, Quebec; in Southeast Asia by Y.W. Ong, 9 Lorong 36 Geylang, Singapore 14; in Australia and the south Pacific by Pet Imports Pty. Ltd., P.O. Box 149, Brookvale 2100, N.S.W., Australia. Published by T.F.H. Publications, Inc. Ltd., The British Crown Colony of Hong Kong.

WHAT IS A SALAMANDER?

Have you ever walked in the woods in the spring and heard the strange voices of the frogs; and have you seen the small slinky creatures that looked like lizards? Of course, you know the difference between a frog and a toad, a salamander and a newt, a skink and a lizard. But we have, in America, England and just about every country that has any water, small animals that live on land or in the pools, ponds and small streams that are to be found all about. These animals, the frogs, toads and salamanders, are truly harmless creatures! They never bite and their only means of defense is in camouflage and a fast retreat.

Though you can find exceptions to every rule, especially the following one, there is one group of animals that is specially adapted to spend part of their lives on land and the rest in the water. They are all cold-blooded animals and we call them *amphibians*. What happens most of the time is that the amphibians breed in or near the water and their young live in the water and go through a stage that we identify as the *tadpole* stage. After the young reach a certain stage in their development, they leave the water and become land animals until they return to the water to breed.

Amphibians are divided into two groups: those with tails are called *tailed amphibians* and those without tails are *tailless amphibians*. The tailless amphibians, the frogs and toads, only have tails in the tadpole stage. The tails are then absorbed as the youngsters mature and the rest of their lives they are tailless. This booklet is not about frogs and toads, but about the tailed amphibians, the most popular of which we call *salamanders*.

If the salamander is lucky and no one (human or animal) bites or cuts off his tail, he will have a tail all his life. That's why we call him a tailed amphibian. However, lizards also have tails all their lives, why are

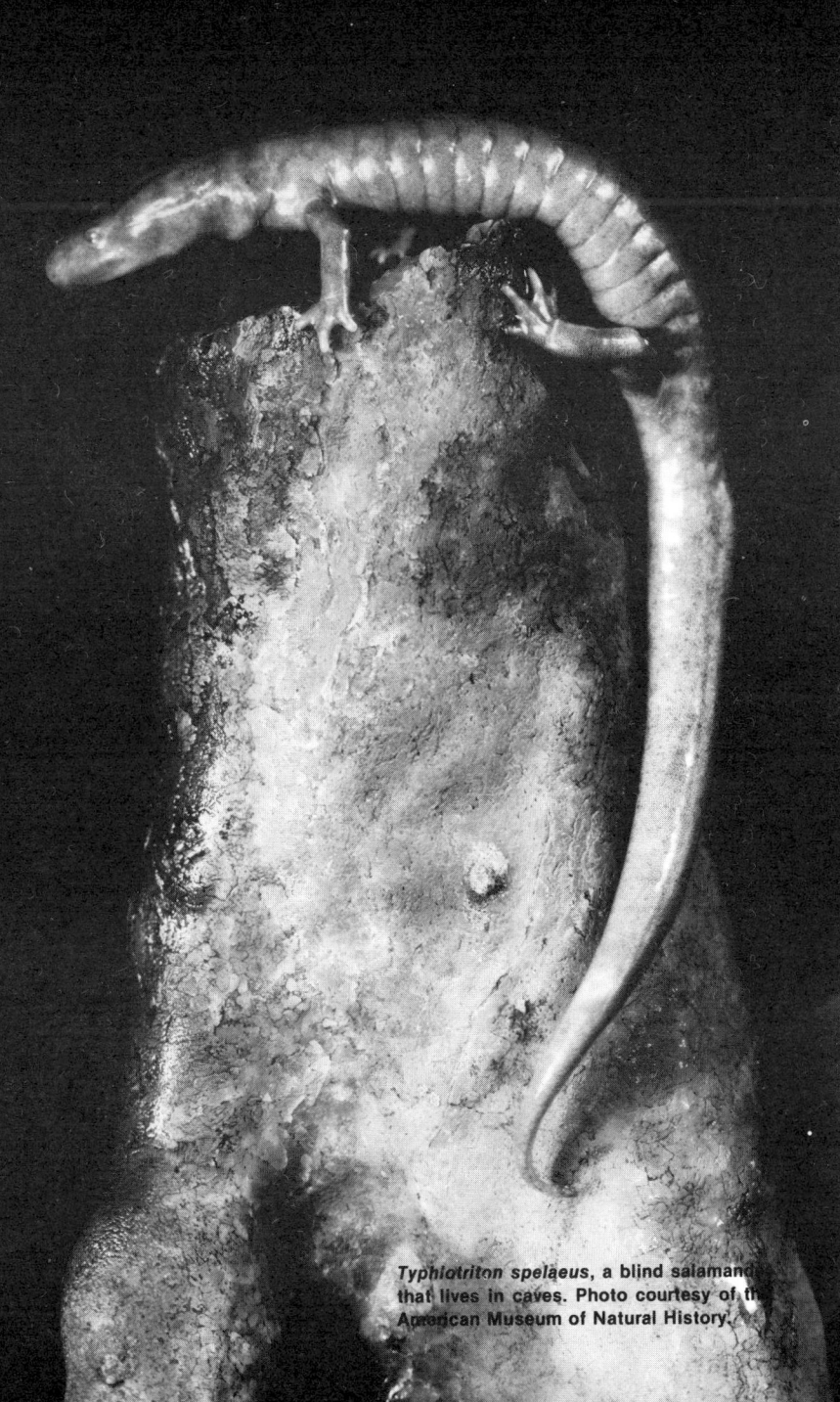

Typhlotriton spelaeus, a blind salamander that lives in caves. Photo courtesy of the American Museum of Natural History.

Plethodon glutinosus, popularly known as the Slimy Salamander. Photo by F.J. Dodd.

they not amphibians? Well, lizards are different than salamanders, and the fact that they live on land has little to do with it [because there is a cute salamander called the Red Back which lives on the land all its life cycle. It lays its eggs in a small bunch in a hole in a log or tree (one that is usually decomposing).] The skin on the lizard is covered with scales and is hard and dry while the skin of a salamander is always soft and slightly moist to the touch. A newt is a particular kind of salamander. A lizard and a salamander are very different.

WHAT IS A NEWT?

Some people call newts *efts*. All newts are salamanders. Often after a cool, spring rain you can see brightly colored salamanders with carmine orange spots running along small paths and roads in the forests and bushes. You rarely see them except after a rain because they must have moisture all around them or they will dry out and die. Many old people will try to tell you that it rains "lizards and newts." Just smile when they tell you that because what actually happens is that these small animals hide and wait until it is wet enough for them to travel and they only come out from hiding when it is raining or when the grass and ground are still wet from a heavy rain.

THE RED-SPOTTED NEWT

Newts have some very interesting characteristics. First of all, many of the same species are very different, yet they will all look alike in general appearance. It is simple to describe one species of them as having a tangerine colored body with vermilion dots on each side of their back. These reddish spots are surrounded by tiny black markings and it is not rare that these black markings appear all over their body. So different are they that many of them have more red marks on

The European Fire Salamander, *Salamandra salamandra*, is boldly patterned and very attractive. This species has been recorded to have lived for over forty years in captivity. Photo by G. Marcuse.

one side of their body than the other . . . some rare specimens may even have no spots on one side, with plenty on the other. They are truly remarkable creatures.

Their faces are interesting too. For noses they merely have tiny pinholes which serve as nostrils. Their eyes are very beautiful in a peculiar sort of way. First of all their eyes are black with pupils that are long and narrow instead of being circular like most animals. The pupils run parallel to the ground and have a magnificent golden band running above and below the black pupil. These golden bands are the iris of the eye.

So small are the feet and legs of this queer animal that it looks like they can hardly move at all, but they are fast and sure. Their front feet have four toes each and their hind feet each have five toes. The shape of the toes on the front feet are much slimmer than those on the hind, as different as our fingers and toes! One interesting characteristic of newts is that their legs are most slim where they join the body and they get heavier as they reach the toes. Just the opposite of the more familiar animals.

The tail of the newt is used like a monkey's tail, for grasping, and it is peculiarly adapted by being completely flat on both sides. Unlike the monkey's tail, however, the newt also uses it for locomotion and for righting itself if it falls or is tossed onto its back. The way the newt walks is very interesting. They walk the way you would walk on your hands and knees. First they put one front foot out and then the rear foot on the opposite side, always utilizing a pair of opposite limbs. If they should stop for some reason and then continue on, their rythm is never broken and they will continue just where they left off, first right then left. They never make use of two right front feet one time after another.

The Red-backed Salamander, *Plethodon cinerens*, with its nest.

WHAT NEWTS EAT

There are big newts and there are small newts and without any doubt you would feed big newts big things and small newts small things. What are these things? Well, probably the best food for all concerned (easy for you to get and for the newt to catch) are worms. Use tiny worms for baby newts and larger garden worms for larger newts. If you happen to have a plant in your home or garden that is infested with plant lice, don't waste your money on expensive sprays and poisons. Just put the plant and the newt in a terrarium and in a few days there won't be any plant lice around at all. Newts consider plant lice a delicacy and they would rather eat them than just about anything else. It is interesting to note that they sneak up on the plant lice, even though the louse has no idea of the imminent danger that lies ahead. And with a motion that is too quick for the eye to follow, they snap the louse up in one gulp and swallow it just as quickly.

The European species *Triturus alpestris,* the Alpine Newt. The male (upper) shows the crest typical of males of this species. Photo by G. Marcuse.

If a newt hasn't seen a plant louse for a few days and he finally discovers one, his elation is beyond description. One day I was teaching a class in biology at New York University. I had a habit of placing aquaria and terraria all about the classroom so my students might learn a little more about animal life than they find in books. I found a small plant that had lice on it so I put the plant in with my small red newt. As soon as he discovered the lice, he danced and pranced all about the plant, as though he was about to mate with another newt, but he was the sole inhabitant of the aquarium-terrarium. Finally, after ten minutes of dancing and admiring his discovery, he developed a beautiful hue and started his meal. So entranced was my class (and myself) that we spent half an hour talking about the habits of these wonderful little creatures. A few weeks later I discovered that nearly half the class had set up their own terraria and had collected their own specimens. (This is one of the few rewards we teachers get from our profession!)

THE LIFE CYCLE OF THE RED-SPOTTED NEWT

All stories begin with the egg and we find the Red-spotted Newt's egg laid on a water plant like *Elodea* or *Myriophyllum* in some little lake, pool, pond or stream. The egg is very tiny, about the size of a sweet pea seed; it is adhesive and sticks to the bushy plant on which it was laid. It looks yellowish because its center contains a kind of yolk. Its protective outer shell is a tough, transparent coating and contains a sort of mucilage which holds the developing eggs fast to the weeds. It may take a month for the eggs to hatch (depending upon the temperature of the water) and what comes out of the egg is very disappointing. The sides are decorated with gray stripes and its gills stick out of the gill slits in back of its head. Its tail is long and skinny and

A larval Tiger Salamander, *Ambystoma tigrinum*, with the branched gills showing very plainly. Photo by R. Zukal.

The light-colored nodules visible on the sides and underjaw of this Crested Newt are glands that produce a slime that protects the newt from drying out when it leaves the water and is exposed to air. Photo by G. Marcuse.

Salamander eggs (an enlarged view).

the newborn newt uses it in swimming. Its swimming ability is amazing and it gets around with no trouble at all. The gills help it to breathe under water and it acts just like a fish, never having to come to the surface for air. As it gets older the colors change until its back is a dull green and its belly is light tan. In a few months it begins to lose its gills, while at the same time small limbs begin to sprout from its smooth sides. In no time at all its gills are gone and by the middle of the summer the green color changes to a bright orange and the newt leaves the water. Most of the time the newt, at this stage, remains hidden under wet leaves or moss, or among the damp ferns. It is only when it rains that the newt can really let himself go, for the only thing that really worries a newt is lack of water: if their skin or gills dry out they will die!

The main reason newts go out in the rain is to hunt for food and though they really don't need a lot of food to live, what they require is very important. Their chief diet is, as we said before, small insects and worms. A newt lives on land for more than two years and some have been found many miles from any water which

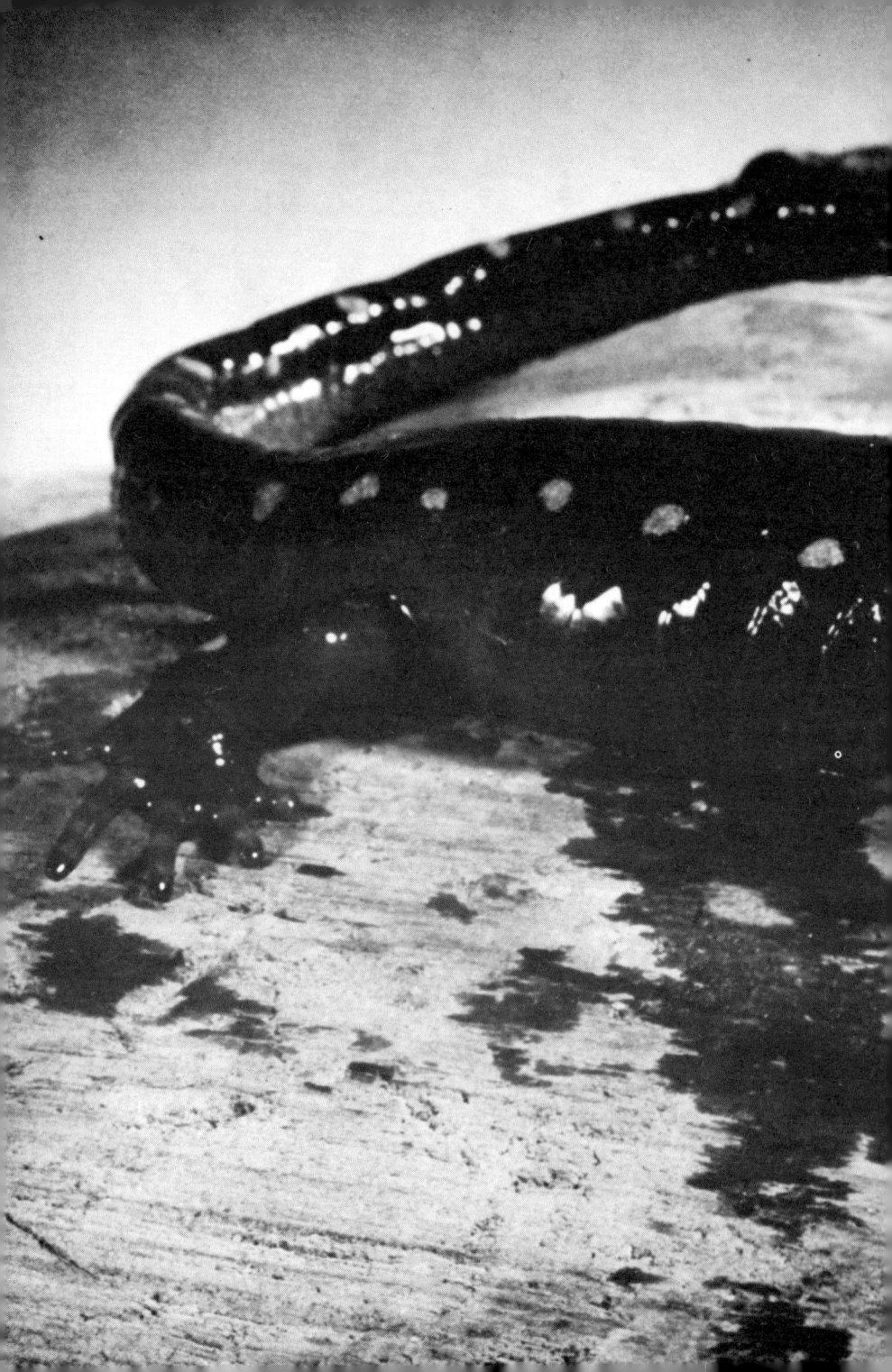

Salamanders are among the most colorful of all animals that can be kept as pets, some of them showing beautiful patterns of starkly contrasting colors. The spots on the back of this Common Spotted Salamander (*Ambystoma maculatum*) are a bright yellow, contrasting vividly with the dark bluish-black back.

This is a male Palmate Newt, *Triturus helveticus*. Note the webbed hind feet and the filament on the tail. Photo by Laurence E. Perkins.

was suitable for them to live in. After this time, usually in their third season, the newt will return to the water where they change colors back to the green back and brown belly. Their tails grow an extended edge which makes it more effective for swimming.

For some reason their legs undergo a slight change and the male's legs become very thick and heavy, while the female's legs seem to become a wee bit slimmer and they are much slighter than the male's.

In the water they seek a mate and lay their eggs in the spring among the many weeds which are found close to the shore in a small pool or pond.

Thus we know the life-story of one of Nature's wonders — the Red-spotted Newt. An animal that not only lives on land and water, but sheds its coat like a snake and then turns around and eats it!

Though not every newt or salamander has the exact same life history as this friendly fellow, the Red-spotted Newt, many have very similar stories. You had best go out to buy a few and set them up in your home so you can study them.

HOW TO STUDY NEWTS AND SALAMANDERS IN YOUR HOME

Before you buy or collect your own newt, obtain an aquarium. You can buy the aquarium at any petshop. Ask the man to give you the largest, flattest kind you can afford. Then buy a reflector for the top of the aquarium so you can have a light to see your salamanders at night. Also buy a hood or piece of glass to put over the top of the aquarium so the water doesn't evaporate and so the salamanders don't escape.

Put in some gravel and a few plants. One or two stones on the bottom will help (see the colored photograph on the cover.) Have a large rock protruding out of the water so your salamander won't drown if he passes into the air-breathing stage while in your aquar-

Non-larval salamanders must be provided with access to atmospheric air or they will drown; here a *Triturus vulgaris* individual comes to the surface of its aquarium to replenish its air supply. Photo by G. Marcuse.

ium. If you get young ones in the spring chances are that by the middle of August they will become terrestrial and will prefer living in a damp place than in water. When this happens remove most of the water from the aquarium and bank the sand so that those salamanders that want the water can stay in it but those that want land can have some land to walk on.

This is an ideal setup for newts and fishes. Water only fills half the aquarium, and rocks jut out to act as perches for those salamanders which want to leave the water. Photo by Perkins.

The photographs show how this type of aquarium can be set up. Get a few bog plants from your florist, or better yet, go to the nearest swamp or damp marsh and get yourself some moss and ferns and plant them in your aquarium. Keep the cover on so that the moisture stays in. You can keep your pets alive and healthy in this aquarium-terrarium for many years, and they will probably breed right before your very eyes!

In the aquarium, your newts and salamanders can be fed tubifex worms which you can get at most petshops. Your aquarium can also contain goldfish or tropical fish

Salamanders have many enemies and are preyed upon by many different animals—but they are not always on the receiving end of predation. Here an adult salamander is swallowing a frog tadpole that it has captured. Photo by Hans Pfletschinger.

for they get along very well with the salamanders (though salamanders may try to swallow any newborn fish if you have livebearing tropical fishes).

SOME INTERESTING VARIETIES—WHERE TO FIND THEM AND HOW THEY LIVE

The Red-spotted Newt, *Triturus viridescens*, is very common in the Eastern United States. The life history of this animal was used as an illustration for the whole group, but it is only fair to state that this was an ideal situation. Some scientists have discovered that the Red-spotted Newt doesn't always leave the water! Sometimes they spend their whole lives in the water. Then, too, sometimes they return to the water after one winter instead of two! What variable animals they are!

The Red Salamander, *Pseudotriton ruber*, is an ideal subject for the aquarium-terrarium. They look a lot like the Red-spotted Newt as they too have black spots on them and they may confuse you. This species, when in the red stage, is about an inch or more longer than the Red-spotted Newt when it is red. (When both are green, after returning to the water, they may grow to about six inches in length.)

The breeding habits of this species is very interesting. Their eggs are fastened together with a long strong sticky substance in bunches about a dozen or two to the strand. As many as five strands are laid. The eggs are usually attached by the string to a rock which is located in a fairly strong current of water so that fresh, cool water is always rushing against the eggs bringing them oxygen and cleaning them off constantly. If you have them in an aquarium you must arrange an air pump with an air stone in such a manner that the bubbles from the stone are constantly agitating the eggs.

The Red Salamander, *Pseudotriton ruber*.

The eggs stay this way all summer and they hatch in September. The young larvae remain inactive all through the long winter and in the spring they suddenly come to life as vicious killers! They attack every small living thing they come across, whether it be a shrimp, worm, snail or small fish. Small bits of meat will do if nothing else is available.

After a few years, they lose their external gills and change from a dull brown to a bright red. Then they leave the water. At the land stage of their development they can be fed bits of meat, earthworms, tubifex worms, plant lice, small bits of juicy liver or meal worms. These salamanders do not have lungs and they use gills which must always be moist, so don't let them dry out or they will surely die.

You can find this species from New York to Georgia and westward to the Mississippi River.

The Dusky Salamander, *Desmognathus fuscus*, is another very common amphibian which is to be found east of the Mississippi River as far north as Canada. The adult form is about 5 inches long with a deep rust colored back and gray belly. There are two irregular

A pair of Crested Newts, male below. Males of this species (*Triturus cristatus*) develop a crest on the back during breeding season, at which time they are easily distinguished from females of the species. Outside the breeding season, however, males do not show the crest or show it in such a reduced stage of development that the difference in appearance between them and the females is much less noticeable. Photo by G. Marcuse.

Demsognathus fuscus carolinensis. On the right is the red cheeked phase; to the left is the usual coloration.

rows of black dots on the top part of the body. The eggs are milky in color and they are laid in nests containing about 20 eggs. The male has been credited with the incubation of the eggs, for he is always lying about them with his body touching them most of the time. It is more likely that he is guarding the eggs for the author has taken the eggs away from the male and hatched them just as successfully as when the eggs were left with the male. Of course this experiment was conducted in an aquarium-terrarium and in Nature things might be a little different.

It takes about two months for the eggs to hatch indoors, (they are laid out of, but very close to, water) and the young stay on land for about two weeks. Most of the eggs are laid in July and August and the young hatch and go to the water in September and October. They stay in the water until the following May or June when they come out to breed.

This is not a very desirable species for the aquarium or terrarium because they hide so much and dig up the

An Axolotl, the albino form. This is an immature form which will lose its external gills and become a land animal. However, mysteriously enough, this group may actually spawn while in the "immature" form. Photo by L. E. Perkins.

Normal forms of Axolotls. Photo by Perkins.

The Giant Salamander with eggs.

The female Palmate Newt in an aquarium, preparing to lay her eggs on a branch of pondweed, *Elodea*. Perkins photo.

A male Smooth Newt, *Triturus vulgaris*. Isn't he a handsome fellow? Photograph by Laurence E. Perkins.

The Spotted Salamander, *Ambystoma maculatum*.

plants. Their jaws are hinged on the bottom with their upper jaw fixed. They stick their jaws under small rocks and open their mouths forcing the rocks over, in their search for food. They seem to always be toppling the moss into the water and throwing the small pebbles about in their search for food. They will dig right into the dirt for small worms, beetles and snails. Most of their time is spent in seclusion.

Another fellow with habits very similar to the Dusky Salamander is the Purple Salamander, *Gryinophilus porphyriticus*, the champion terrarium wrecker around. In his quest for food he completely disorganizes the turf, rocks and gravel. Their chief attraction is their reddish purple color, but their untidy habits are very discouraging for the beginner.

The Japanese Newt, *Molge pyrrhogastra*, is perhaps the most familiar newt around the world. Every year millions of these small animals are sold in petshops, 5 & 10¢ stores and variety stores all over the country, but strange at it may seem this variety is imported from Japan.

The size of this species is about four inches long with a dark back, sometimes dark enough to be called black, while its belly is bright red. Its backbone sticks out instead of having the usual dorsal crest.

A Cave Salamander, *Eurycea lucifuga*. The back of this salamander is red or orange, irregularly marked with dark brown or black spots. This a head-on view.

This variety is imported because they are very hardy, take food readily, and are not shy.

The Tiger Salamander, *Ambystoma tigrinum*, is so named because of the yellow bars on a rusty black body. This species is nocturnal in habits —— and it is rare that you find them about during the day. This species is found in just about every state in the Union.

All *Ambystoma tigrinum* (Tiger Salamanders) begin their intriguing life as the Red-spotted Salamander did, as an egg. They grow up in the water and have the feathery gills which earned them the distinction of being considered as a different species than the adult. They called the larval form of the salamander an *Axolotl* and it wasn't until 1865 when they had some of these larvae on display in Paris, that they discovered that this "species" was merely the larval form of a very familiar salamander.

Since the Tiger Salamander spends most of his time buried in the mud and under plants, don't expect too much amusement from him.